Managing and Understanding Parental Anger

The Coping Parent Series:

Managing and Understanding Parental Anger _____

Harriet H. Barrish, Ph.D.
I.J. Barrish, Ph.D.

Foreword by
Albert Ellis, Ph.D.

Revised edition

Westport Publishers, Inc.
Kansas City, Missouri

Cover by: Ken Walker and Matt Moore
Text layout by Noelle M. Kaplan, finedesign

ISBN 0-933701-41-1 (previously ISBN 0-930851-02-1)

Printed in the United States of America

Library of Congress Cataloging-in-Publication Data

Barrish, Harriet H., 1945-
    Managing and understanding parental anger/Harriet H. Barrish,
I.J. Barrish. — Rev. ed.
        p.   cm. — (The Coping parent series)
    Includes bibliographical references.
    ISBN 0-933701-41-1: $6.95
    1. Parenting.   2. Discipline of children.   3. Anger.   4. Rational-emotive
    psychotherapy.   5. Self-help techniques.   I. Barrish,
    I.J., 1945- .   II. Title.   III. Series.
HQ755.8.B376   1989   89-22503
649' .1 '019—dc20   CIP

Dedicated to our children,
Bradley, Jonas, and Brandy,
who endure our anger from time to time.

Table of Contents

Foreword

Although there have been scores of books written on anger and hundreds more on parenting, I know of no good one other than this that adequately deals with managing parental anger. The Roman philosopher, Seneca, was perhaps the first writer to devote a whole book to showing people how to eliminate anger; and the Greek-Roman Stoic, Epictetus, also showed how it could be eliminated.

Not so most modern psychotherapists! Believing in the Freudian hydraulic theory of the emotions — which holds that if you suppress strong feelings, like anger, they still unconsciously grip you and will inevitably rise to smite you again — these therapists urge you to express and release your anger, wrongly assuming that it will then go away. Since I originated it in 1955, rational-emotive therapy (RET) has taught millions of clients and readers how to admit that they create their enraged feelings and that they can almost invariably overcome them. My own books — especially *A New Guide To Rational Living* and *Anger: How To Live With And Without It* have pioneered in this respect; and other RET books, such as Paul Hauck's *Overcoming Frustration and Anger* have followed suit.

Now Harriet and Jay Barrish have made a trailbreaking attempt to show parents how to cope with their own and their children's anger. And a fine attempt it is! Using their original skills in behavior therapy and adding to them the skills of RET (which is the most popular form of cognitive-behavior therapy), they have put together a large number of helpful suggestions for angry parents. They show parents how to dispute their anger-creating irrational beliefs; how to use rational coping statements in their stead; how to discipline their children without anger; how to help each other surrender their harmful rage; how to accept themselves and their children unconditionally; and how to effectively use many of the main techniques of RET to overcome their own and their offspring's anxiety and depression, as well as anger.

I am delighted to see this unique parenting manual in print and predict that it will be of immense value to many parents — and probably of even more help to their no longer suffering children!

Albert Ellis, Ph.D.
Institute for Rational-Emotive Therapy
New York, New York

Preface

This is a book about and for normal, well-meaning, conscientious, loving, educated parents who get ANGRY. You know the type, you've seen them at school, in the neighborhood, at the restaurant, at the grocery store or pool. Your best friend is probably one and so are you. We're the reasonable and rational ones who are suddenly transformed into grouchy, critical, snapping people who say things we wish we hadn't or we feel trapped into doing things we didn't want to do.

We all experience anger at one time or another in the course of parenting. Sometimes more frequently than at other times; sometimes more intensely than at other times. There are lots of "reasons why" for anger. Parenting is probably one of the most time-consuming, energy-consuming, expensive responsibilities we will ever embark upon, yet most of us are ill-prepared for the things we will encounter. We have not been formally taught the skills to parent nor the skills to cope as parents. Some of us were fortunate to have good parent models, but some of us were not. Most parents find themselves using their own judgment, based on what seems to make sense or based on a definite opinion about what their own parents did that was right or wrong. Many parents continue to blindly react to situations with little insight as to why they are making certain choices or with little concern about how appropriate these choices are and what results these choices will have for both parent and child.

Parents today who are in their 20's and 30's are finding increasing access to books, courses, and workshops that teach general parenting skills or that deal with particular issues that arise at certain developmental stages in children. These courses and literature do not arise out of perceived need and concern; to be available and to multiply as they have, they require consumers, and our generation is indeed one of parenting consumers. Private practitioners, mental health centers, hospitals, agencies, schools, PTAs, and special interest groups are all involved in the parenting business, and we must learn to become critical consumers. One element which does appear important to parents is whether they can use the information and skills they have acquired in parenting a child. Without effective parenting skills, some parents quickly resort to anger because there seems to be no other options.

Good parenting skills are not the only variables which affect parental anger. We, as parents, also bring into the parent-child relation a personal tendency for temperament and skills in handling our own frustration and upsets. Anger is such a personal tendency. We find fertile ground in our lives for unresolved and building resentments involving personal life goals, marital relations, business goals and relations, economic status, and garden variety everyday stresses. None of these are left at the doorstep when we suddenly switch into the parent role. The anger and accumulating resentments spill over into parenting. Suddenly we feel trapped into being the bad-guy parent who is a disciplinarian-enforcer to a resistant kid. Our intolerance is a more frequent or intense occurrence.

And then there are the kids. Beautiful kids. Energetic kids. Wonderful, lovable, nerve-wracking kids. Challenging kids, demanding kids. Uncooperative and angry kids. Imitating kids...professionals long ago gave up the idea of kids being miniature adults, but have parents? Children have their own child ideas and notions, yet as parents we often require and **demand** that they march to our music. The problem, of course, comes when the child is playing a different tune than the parent. Part of our role as parents includes socializing and teaching our child what the rules of the game are, but sometimes we lose sight of the fact that the rules are made for potential violators. Rules are broken as a part of the learning process. It is to be expected of children.

While there are lots of reasons why there is anger in parenting, this book will try to emphasize how to manage anger. We will be addressing parenting skills, with an emphasis on the skills needed to cope as parents. Parents frequently view anger as being outside their control because, after all, other people or situations cause our anger. As parents, we can easily feel like the victim. While most of us have overtly made the choice to become parents, we frequently feel the new responsibility is unfair or is not what we expected. We are presented with an ever-changing family system which develops new patterns and does not allow for a return to the old husband-wife system. Through a common process of projecting blame on everything and everyone else, we feel like "victims" and soon develop negative feelings about parenting.

By implementing the suggestions discussed in this book, which is based on the pioneering work of Dr. Albert Ellis, you can learn to feel better about your kids, your parenting, and yourselves. You can be in more control than you realize. It begins by placing the responsibility for upset and anger where it really lies —with ourselves. It is then and only then that we can begin the process of managing our parental anger. By doing this you can also begin to question the value of continuing in the same victim path. As you will see, there certainly are disadvantages to the victim course and anger — the biggest disadvantage is that parenting can become unpleasant and non-rewarding. Parenting is **not** a one-way process. Good parenting requires that both parent and child find the relation rewarding.

Acknowledgements

In working with parents and families for numerous years it became apparent to us that just teaching parents what to do about their youngster's behavior sometimes did not work. The continuing problem was that often negative parental emotions such as anger interfered with the use of the vast assortment of available behavioral management strategies.

About the same time as the realization that other parental skills were needed, we became familiar with a newly emerging approach to managing emotional and behavioral responses. Our realization of rational emotive therapy's (RET) tremendous potential for being integrated with behavioral management procedures led to this book being written.

The main ideas developed in this book concerning management of anger, self-downing and self-worth come from rational emotive therapy and its founder Dr. Albert Ellis. Through the Institute for Rational Emotive Therapy in New York and its fine staff, we were fortunate to develop extensive skills in the use of rational emotive therapy. As these skills were being refined we began to integrate rational emotive therapy with more traditional behavioral procedures.

We have been nurtured by so many people in the process of this book becoming a reality. First, Dr. Albert Ellis has offered continuing suggestions and assistance. Drs. Albert Ellis, Richard Wessler, Raymond DiGiuseppe, Virginia Walters, William Golden, Rose

Oliver, Ruth Wessler, and Janet Wolfe were all vital in the development of our rational emotive therapy skills. Second, the Departments of Human Development and Psychology at the University of Kansas, and in particular our academic advisors, Drs. Donald M. Baer and Montrose Wolf, provided training, support, and guidance in behavioral psychology and behavioral management. We wish to acknowledge a debt of gratitude to a number of other professionals who were helpful at a number of stages in our professional development: Drs. Rogers Elliot, Marvin Fine, Kris Guest, Frances Degan Horowitz, L. Keith Miller, Jan Roosa, Maynard Shelley, James Sherman, and James Stachowiak. Our professional colleague at the University of Kansas Medical Center, Dr. Edward Christophersen, also served as a continuing supporter and source of guidance during the process. Further our friend, clinical supervisor, and colleague, Dr. Gerald Vandenberg, always gave us excellent feedback, support, and caring in our activities. We also acknowledge a debt of gratitude to Ann Wilke, who assisted in rewriting of this manuscript so it would be more readable for parents, Barbara Cochrane, who provided editorial assistance, and Jeanne Malone, who assisted in preparation of the manuscript. We also appreciated the counsel and guidance of Sidney L. Willens. Last but not least, we express our love and gratitude to our nurturing parents, Ruth and Leo Shultz, Betty Nadlman, and to Charles Nadlman and Joseph Barrish, of blessed memory.

Introduction

Picture the modern parent: well-meaning and well-read, concerned with loving their offspring, an ordinary sort pushing the grocery cart, waiting at a McDonald's counter, peering from the bathroom mirror.

Now color this rational adult ANGRY: anything from gray for grouchiness to red for rage will do.

The transformation is a common one. It happens to us as parents with varying degrees of intensity and frequency. For some, its expression is an outburst of arm-flinging and door-slamming; for others, a cold glare and single biting remark speak the message.

Anger can turn the most reasonable, caring parent among us into a snapping, snarling critic. Unplanned words and acts escape, trailing regret and guilt. Gaps widen and walls go up.

Our anger springs from many sources: frustration at our lack of parenting skill, the upsets from other segments of our lives, unrealized expectations of our children and our relationship with them.

Anger is as much a part of parenting as wet diapers. Most of us, however, are better prepared to handle the wet diapers than our own angry feelings. And that is part of the problem. We are ill-prepared for the time-, energy- and dollar-consuming responsibilities of parenthood. A few of us had exceptional role models in our parents, but who was paying attention then? Most of us stumble through the parenting process with a mixture of instinct, judgment, inherited opinion, and the deep hope that everything will somehow turn out all right.

Heightened awareness of our lack of parenting skill has spawned a whole industry — books, workshops, seminars — designed for the parenting consumer. Everyone from private practitioner to PTA group is getting in on the act. We rush to digest the information and are often disappointed or confused.

Can we apply the experts' suggestions to the day-to-day challenge of rearing our children? If we cannot, if the "how-to" skills elude us, then we are apt, in our frustration, to resort to anger because we feel that it is all we have left.

Frustration with lack of practical, hands-on parenting knowledge is one source of our anger. Daily life is fertile ground for growing resentments. Marital concerns, personal defeats, business problems, economic fears — all take a toll. We don't have a neat little package of cares that we can leave outside when we step into our parenting role. The anger born from those sources spills out, self-control lessens, and the classic confrontation results: bad-guy parent vs. resisting kid.

And what about the kids? What do they do that sets us off? What do we expect from them?

Children are not miniature adults. We've been told that before, but sometimes we have a hard time remembering it. Children have their own ideas. No matter how firm our demands or how inspiring our lead, they will, from time to time, march to their own tunes. And so they should.

Part of our job as parents is teaching the rules of the game to our children. Rules are, after all, make for potential violators. Breaking them is part of learning and should be expected. Yet, in the face of shattered rules and defiant acts, our anger can build up.

Enough about the "why's" of parental anger. What we need is some "why not's," and some managing skills. That's what this book is about.

As we have learned from Dr. Albert Ellis' approach to upset, angry feelings are something we can choose to have or not to have and, yes, anger can be managed.

Step one in the management training is an admission: **the responsibility for our anger is within ourselves** — not out there somewhere on the shoulders of other people and situations. True, the parent status changes life, poses new restrictions, and presents some unforeseen challenges. If we continue to blame outside sources for our anger, however, we slip into the role of "permanent victim," a sticky, self-defeating and unhappy position with few rewards.

When we recognize our own responsibility for our anger, we are on the way. That which is within us is within our control. With the acquisition and practice of some basic skills, we can learn to manage the anger and improve the parenting experience — for our children and for ourselves.

You can begin the relearning process by learning to say helpful things to yourself immediately. This book will help you to do this by presenting key phrases in the first person, "I". As you begin to read, you will start saying more helpful things to yourself. As we learn from the work of Dr. Ellis, helpful statements are designed to place the responsibility for upset with ourselves in order to more frequently remove us from a victim role and allow us to manage our feelings in the often very difficult situations involved in parenting.

Let's begin...

Chapter 1

Anger: How It Interferes; Getting Angry

Anger Interferes With Successful Parenting

Anger interferes with your ability to make an intelligent decision. Most situations offer you a choice of responses. The heat of anger clouds both your view of options and your capacity to choose the one most appropriate.

Often, too, you direct your parental anger at your children instead of at their inappropriate behavior. The result? A child who withdraws, who stays out of an angry parent's way. Or one who learns to "shape up" to avoid a bad scene. The chance for that child to recognize his or her inappropriate behavior and try to correct it is lost. Often, phrases such as, "I'm a bad parent/bad person," or "This parenting business is for the birds!" results. Bad feelings about yourself and the parenting process are common post-anger feelings. No one enjoys being the bad guy.

The parent who uses anger to discipline justifies that action: "My children only pay attention to me when I get angry" or "What else can I do when they act like that?" Learning about the nature of anger and some ways to manage it can help you to see the weakness of those rationales. **Most** of the time, you do have a choice; **most** of the

1

time, anger is not your only option.

It is important to realize the distinction between **nonhurtful** and **hurtful** anger. Parents can be effective when dealing with their children while annoyed, irritated or aggravated. Keeping parental anger at this level is considered nonhurtful anger. Parents experiencing nonhurtful anger can educate, problem solve and be assertive while focusing on the child's judgments and actions. Kids can more easily "hear" when parents approach them at this level because the child won't be likely to feel the need to become defensive or reactive.

When anger goes beyond aggravation and begins to move into internal hurt or expressed aggression it is considered hurtful anger. When parents are hurtfully angry they tend to be reactive focusing on the child as a person rather than the misaction or misjudgment. Hurtful anger can lead to emotional abuse, name calling and even physical aggression. Hurtful anger can also lead to escalating conflict between family members, low self-esteem, guilt and anxiety.

Through a new perspective and some practice, you can learn to:
1. **anticipate** the anger-breeding situation and prepare yourself for a calm response;
2. **recognize** your angry reaction in progress and calm yourself down quickly;
3. **review** your behavior (after an incident is over) objectively so that you can learn from it for the next situation.

You can learn to help yourself and your children. You can learn the self-statements and behaviors that will often make your parental anger more manageable.

Some sections of this book begin with a key helpful statement (or statements).

Children Do Misbehave.
My Children Will Misbehave.

Children misbehave. So it is and so it will be. That is why rules exist.

Rules are guidelines; they tell children what to do and what not to do. Rules remind parents what behaviors need consistent enforcement.

When a rule is broken, you should provide a negative consequence. When no rules are being broken — when, in fact, rules are being followed — provide positive consequences so your children know the behavior is acceptable, even commendable. CATCH THEM BEING GOOD. For example, when Johnny takes out the trash as asked, it would be preferable to have his Mom or Dad positively notice by saying "Johnny, I really like the way you take care of your chores by taking out the trash." Another example would be if Robby brings home his homework and immediately sits down to do it, rather than putting it off. His Mom or Dad might say, "Robby, I really like the responsibility you are showing by getting your work done right away rather than putting it off." Further his parents could show their interest in his homework by actively listening and encouraging his homework behavior.

When My Children Misbehave, Their Misbehavior Does Not Cause My Anger. I Cause My Anger By The Way I View The Misbehavior.

If it is truly your children's misbehavior that upsets you, then you are indeed doomed to a life of anger. Whenever your child misbehaves, you will become angry. You will be a permanent victim.

Can that be true? Think for a minute. Do you **always** get angry **every time** your children misbehave? No, you don't. The antics that "make" you angry this morning may not "make" you angry this afternoon; today's misbehaviors get quite a different reaction from yesterday's.

Why is that? Why does the same misbehaving act seem more important one time than it does another? Circumstances change. Sometimes you are more tired than at other times, sometimes your outlook is bright because your day has been good. Some days you feel more kind to your spouse or to yourself and thus, your tolerance for your kid's behavior is increased.

The point is this — the misbehavior did not cause the anger. The way you regarded that misbehavior — for whatever reason — is what caused the anger. And that is good news. That means you can place yourself in a position of control over your anger.

When My Children Misbehave, I Will Make Myself Angry If I Regard Their Misbehavior In Any Of The Following Non-Helpful Ways:

1. My children SHOULD NOT, MUST NOT or CANNOT act this way.
2. When my children behave this way, they are doing it TO me and they deserve to be punished.
3. My children SHOULD know better.
4. It's TERRIBLE and AWFUL when my children behave this way.
5. I CAN'T STAND IT when my children behave this way.
6. People think I am a bad parent or person when my children behave this way.
7. I am a BAD PARENT or PERSON when my children behave this way.
8. I HAVE TO get angry to make my children stop acting this way.

None of these are helpful thoughts; some are downright damaging. Yet they are common self-statements and they need some realistic examination.

Remember: children DO misbehave. They are not born with a knowledge of all "parental rules." Even if they were, they would not consistently live by those rules any more than you would. Like parents, children are fallible. They will make mistakes and errors in judgment.

So — it is NOT terrible and awful when a child misbehaves unless you convince yourself it is terrible and awful. The misbehavior of children is a predictable fact of life. Period.

The idea that you CAN'T STAND your children's misbehavior is a pretty serious one. Your children WILL misbehave. Does that mean you will not be able to succeed as a parent? What you probably mean is that it is uncomfortable for you when your children misbehave. That discomfort is common for parents. Your level of tolerance — that point before you start screaming —gets low; you are tired, other problems are pressing in upon you. Perhaps you have fallen into the habit of behavior expectations that are too high or too rigid. Then, when the misbehavior happens, you take it personally: "That kid is challenging me — me personally!" Then comes anger.

Sometimes children misbehave and someone nearby throws you a critical look—one that seems to say, "What kind of a parent are you anyway to have produced a child like this?" You make the mistake of thinking those looks count for anything in your life. You equate the misbehavior with a personal putdown; it becomes one more vivid example of your failure as a parent. Others are thinking poorly of you and you believe that you need their approval to be an OK person. Your children's misbehavior has put your own personal worth in jeopardy! How dare they do that!

With thoughts like that, you pave the way for an angry outburst.

In reality, it is UNPLEASANT to have a child misbehave in public, it is EMBARRASSING, and it is not unusual to feel UNCOMFORTABLE at such times. But, you can stand it, you will live through it without any real damage having been done. Virtually every child has acted up in public to the embarrassment of his or her parents and, with no exceptions, the child's parents lived through it.

Chapter 2

Anger: Finding Other Alternatives — Getting Rid of Anger

When My Children Misbehave, I Do Not Have To Like It, Approve It or Condone It, But I Don't Have To Get Angry Either.

Giving up the anger-causing ways you look at your children's misbehavior does not mean you have to ignore, accept or condone that behavior. Quite the opposite.

When your children misbehave, you can provide an appropriate penalty. You can do this **within** the guidelines of good discipline and without anger. The absence of anger does not mean the absence of reacting and consequences.

To educate your children in appropriate and inappropriate behaviors, try to provide positive rewards for appropriate behavior and penalties for inappropriate behavior. Some helpful guidelines for promoting good discipline are included in chapter 5 of this book.

When I Make Myself Angry by Regarding My Children's Behavior in Non-Helpful Ways, I Will Challenge These Non-Helpful Thoughts So That I Can View My Children's Behavior More Helpfully.

Challenging your thoughts is a step-by-step process. IDENTIFY what you are thinking, and RECOGNIZE the non-helpful ways you are viewing your children's behavior. Then CHALLENGE each non-helpful thought by questioning its REASONABLENESS, LIKELIHOOD, PROOF AVAILABLE, EXACTNESS AND HELPFULNESS.

Below we have identified some non-helpful ways of regarding children's behavior. If you have any of those thoughts, you will probably make yourself angry. However, if you challenge each of those statements, you will help yourself to see that none of them are reasonable or likely. Go through these statements, one at a time, to see which ones apply to you. Think each through. Soon you will become aware of helpful ways to regard your children's misbehavior.

Examples of some challenging questions that correspond to our list of non-helpful statements follow. Asking yourself these questions may make you become aware of helpful, rather than non-helpful thoughts.

Non-Helpful Thoughts — Challenges To Non-Helpful Thoughts

1. My children SHOULD NOT, MUST NOT, OR CANNOT act in this manner.
   a. Is it likely that my children will **never** act in this manner?
   b. Is it likely that my children will **never** misbehave?
   c. Do I have evidence that my children **will** probably misbehave (they just did)?
   d. If my children just misbehaved and I continue to demand that they should not, will this way of viewing my children's misbehavior be helpful to me or my children?
   e. Is it reasonable for me to continue to demand that my children will never misbehave?

8

2. When my children behave in this manner, they are doing it TO ME and they deserve to be punished.
   a. Would their behavior look any different if they were just breaking a rule?
   b. Is it helpful to make discipline a personal confrontation or issue?
   c. If behavior is inappropriate, should I provide a negative consequence for their behavior just to get back at my children?
   d. Am I trying to punish the children or their behavior?

3. My children should know better.
   a. Do I have any proof that my children do know better?
   b. If my children do not know better, does it mean that they do not know the rule?
   c. If my children do know better, is it possible they may still make a mistake or a poor choice and break a rule?
   d. Should my children **always** know how to behave?
   e. Should my children **always** make the correct behavior choice?

4. It's terrible and awful when my children behave this way.
   a. Is it as terrible and awful as a world catastrophe, such as famine or flood?
   b. Is it as terrible and awful as a catastrophic childhood disease?
   c. Is it unfortunate, undesirable, or non-enjoyable?

5. I cannot stand it when my children behave this way.
   a. Am I going to die from it?
   b. Am I going to commit suicide over it?
   c. Can I find it unacceptable but still survive it?
   d. Can I be reasonably happy even if my children continue to act this way?

6. People think I am a bad parent or person when my children behave this way.
   a. If other people think this way, does it mean that they are necessarily correct?
   b. Would they think this if my children had not misbehaved? If so are they then reacting to me or only to my

children's behavior?

    c. Is it reasonable for someone to think that children **never** misbehave and therefore the parent must be a bad parent when a child does misbehave?

7. I am a bad parent or person when my children behave this way.
    a. Is it reasonable for me to always have total control over my children?
    b. Is there more to good parenting than whether my children never misbehave?
    c. Will I be as effective as a parent if I feel bad about my role and myself?
    d. Is it possible to be a fairly good parent and still have children who misbehave?

8. I have to get angry in order to make my children stop acting this way.
    a. Is anger the only way to teach children?
    b. Is it possible that there are other ways of disciplining children without anger that I have not learned?
    c. If my children misbehave again, is my anger really stopping them?
    d. Do I have examples of other ways that my children have learned things I wanted them to learn without the use of anger?

What I Say To Myself After My Anger — Hurtful Thoughts —Helpful Thoughts.

Just as I cause my own anger by the way I view my children's misbehavior, so do I cause my own upset and the depression that follows by what I say to myself after my anger.

When I do make myself angry, I will feel upset and depressed if I put myself down with any of the following thoughts:

1. I **should never** make myself angry when my children misbehave.
2. I **should always** remain calm with my children.
3. It's **terrible** and **awful** if I get angry.
4. I **can't stand it** when I behave in an angry manner.

5. I am a basically bad parent if I become angry.
6. I **should** think less of myself when I become angry.
7. Others must think I am a bad parent and person when I become angry.

When I do make myself angry over my children's misbehavior (and occasionally I will), I will help myself as a parent if I actually say to myself the following helpful statements:

1. Since I am a fallible human being who makes mistakes, I will sometimes make myself angry when my children misbehave.
2. It is not reasonable to believe I will always remain calm as a parent.
3. It is unfortunate, too bad, and regrettable when I make myself angry — but it is **not** a catastrophe.
4. I can stand the fact that I made myself angry, but I do not have to approve of it.
5. As a parent, I will make mistakes and sometimes not perform well with my children, but this does not take away my overall worth as a parent.
6. As a person, I will make mistakes and sometimes behave in a less than desirable manner, but this does not take away my worth as a person. I do not have to judge myself as a person when I make a mistake. I made a mistake, **PERIOD!**

When I Have Difficulty Saying Helpful Things To Myself.

Sometimes it will be difficult for me to say helpful things to myself because sometimes it "pays off" to make myself angry.

Sometimes parent anger seems to work. Our children or our mate rewards it and none of us realizes we are falling into a damaging trap.

The trap can work between the parents or between parent and child. Between parent and child, the trap operates like this: the child misbehaves — you get angry — the child stops. At the next incident of misbehavior, you try anger again. Soon you are using anger regularly to make the child do what you want. What has this child learned? Good behavior is only necessary when your parents are angry.

It is tough to give up anger when it seems like such a workable tool or when it appears to be the only way to get the child's attention.

Fact: Other techniques work **better**.

A variation of the same trap happens between the parents. You deliver your anger with your children's misbehavior to your spouse: "Aren't you going to do **something** about that child?" You **demand** action.

Sometimes, it is the angry mother demanding the father's involvement; maybe she is frustrated in dealing with the child or maybe she is upset with her own anger. Or this may be the only tool she feels she has for involving the father in discipline. The father's reaction? He resents the "bad guy-enforcer" role and he resents the child for upsetting everyone. So — soon he is angry, too.

It is tough to give up anger when it seems to be the only way to get a spouse involved in parenting.

Fact: Other techniques work **better**.

Learn to recognize these common family traps and to weigh their emotional costs to you. Is your anger so precious to you that you want to keep it and maintain a family system that helps damage you and your children?

Being More Effective in Angry Situations By Stopping, Thinking, Acting.

I will be more effective as a parent in handling a situation in which I make myself angry if I Stop — Think — Act.

One of the toughest tasks for you as a parent beginning to use the techniques in this book will be breaking that chain of events that happen so quickly when you make yourself angry.

STOP — THINK — ACT: this is a helpful strategy that often works to break that chain. Here's the process:

Learn to recognize the first signs of your anger beginning. The earlier you recognize your own anger pattern the more quickly you can do something about it, and your chances for regaining control are better. If you become aware of your own behavior, you can often spot those specific signals that warn of anger approaching. Phrases (spoken or thought) such as "Oh, no!", "Damn it!", "This is all I need!", "How could you?", "Caught you!", or physiological signs such as a hot flash, a blush, a tightening in the head or chest, setting of the jaw, clenching of a fist, flaring of the nostrils, or increase in breathing rate are clear signals that shout: "TAKE NOTE OF WHAT

IS ABOUT TO HAPPEN."

STOP: STOP this chain from building. **Interrupt the process**. Remove yourself from the situation briefly — either physically or mentally. Walk away for 60 seconds, count to 10 or 20 slowly and take a deep breath. Put on the stereo headphones and listen to some favorite music. Do **something** which will interrupt the buildup of your anger.

THINK: After you have begun to stop the process, use a little more time to THINK about what is happening and what you will do. Ask yourself how you are making yourself angry. What are you saying to yourself about your children's misbehavior to create your upset?

Decide how you would prefer to handle the situation. How would you prefer to be acting? Close your eyes and picture yourself engaging in the preferred behavior.

ACT: Return to the situation and ACT.

STOP — THINK — ACT is not a lengthy process. At first, it may take some time until you get the hang of it. If you practice often, though, the whole process can be completed in a matter of minutes or even seconds.

When My Baby Misbehaves —
Helpful Statements.

If you have an infant, your helpful statements could include statements like these:

When my baby misbehaves by not responding to my efforts and settling down and I am sure he or she is not ill, I will handle the situation better if, after challenging my non-helpful thoughts, I actually say to myself the following helpful statements:

1. My baby **will** misbehave and not cooperate — sometimes more than other times. This is a highly probable fact.
2. My baby will be fussy at times. There may be nothing I can do to quiet my baby, except to gently put him or her in the crib and let him or her cry.
3. It is difficult to listen to my baby cry, but the crying **will** stop and I **can** stand it until then. This has happened before and the crying stopped. I have been able to stand it before.
4. It is unfortunate when my baby misbehaves, but it is not a disaster.
5. It is not enjoyable when my baby is fussy. I do not have to **like** listening to the crying, but I can tolerate it.
6. It is preferable that my baby cooperate, but lack of cooperation is sometimes very probable. I can stand that.
7. When my baby misbehaves and is uncooperative, he or she is just doing what most babies do. PERIOD! This mis-behavior **does not** mean I am a bad parent or person — unless I allow it to mean that.
8. I do NOT have to get angry to get my baby to cooperate. If I am yelling or getting angry often because my baby is uncooperative, perhaps I should have the doctor check my baby's health. Perhaps, also, I need to adjust my expectations about parenting and babies and get some support or professional assistance for my feelings.
9. Sometimes I will get angry. I am, after all, a fallible human being. And I do sometimes set myself up for anger with my own non-helpful thoughts about my baby's behavior.

When My Children Misbehave — Helpful Statements.

When my children misbehave, I will handle the situation better if, after challenging my non-helpful thoughts, I actually say to myself the following helpful statements.

1. My children WILL misbehave. Sometimes more than other times. This is highly probable.
2. When my children misbehave, they have only broken a rule. PERIOD!
3. When my children misbehave, I can be most helpful by giving them a meaningful penalty and then recognizing acceptable behavior. WITHOUT ANGER!
4. My children will make mistakes even if they know the rules.
5. It is unfortunate when my children misbehave, but it is not a disaster.
6. It is not enjoyable when my children misbehave, but it is tolerable.
7. It is preferable that my children behave but it is probable that they won't and I can stand that.
8. When my children misbehave, their behavior is inappropriate and they are breaking a rule. PERIOD! It does not mean I am a bad parent or person unless I ALLOW it to mean this.
9. I do NOT have to get angry to discipline my children. If I find myself repeating warnings or yelling, it means I am not using an effective discipline technique and it would be a good idea to rethink my strategy in this and similar situations.
10. I will at times get angry because I am a fallible human being and I set myself up with inappropriate thoughts about my children's misbehavior.

Chapter 3

Anger: Identifying Specific Hurtful And Helpful Thoughts

Recognizing Hurtful And Helpful Thoughts

It may be helpful for you to make a list of situations which keep happening — starting with those often associated with full-blown anger. You can then begin working with the mild anger situations and gradually move on to more difficult situations using these techniques.

Learning to recognize non-helpful thoughts and to change them to helpful thoughts will assist me to become a more effective parent **before** the situation again arises, **during** an anger-breeding situation, and **after** I have made myself angry.

Using Self-Help Worksheets During And After Angry Situations.

Several self-help worksheets with challenging situations that occur with infants, children and adolescents are included. The situations covered are examples of situations that are often difficult for parents to handle. By reviewing and using these self-help sheets, you can become better at identifying both your non-helpful thoughts and more helpful thoughts. By following the step-by-step self-help sheet instructions, you can improve their ability to deal with anger.

The self-help worksheets can offer you a tool to analyze situations that have **already** been hard to handle. So the next time a similar situation arises you will be able to manage it more successfully. The self-help worksheets also will provide you **during** a difficult situation some help in managing it by having examples of non-helpful and helpful thoughts for you to immediately review.

Using self-help worksheets during an anger-breeding situation:
To use the self-help worksheet during an anger-breeding situation, go to a quiet place to review the self-help form (do not attempt to review while remaining in the anger-breeding situation). Look at the self-help worksheet and begin.
  A. Identify the situation or what happened (1).
  B. Identify how you are feeling (3) and how you are behaving or feel like behaving (4).
  C. Identify what you are thinking to yourself that is not helping you handle the situation better (2).
  D. Identify what you can think to yourself to help you handle the situation better (5).
  E. Identify how you will feel (6) and how you will behave (7), if you begin to think more helpfully.
  F. Identify discipline strategies/alternative parent behavior options for handling the situation.

Using self-help worksheets following an anger-breeding situation:
  A. Identify the situation or what happened (1).
  B   Identify how you felt (3) and what your behavior looked like (4).
  C. Identify what you thought to yourself that did **not** help you handle the situation (2) and led to how you felt (3).
  D. Identify what you can think to yourself to help you handle the situation better (5).
  E. Identify how you can feel (6) and what your behavior can look like (7) if you think more helpfully.
  F. Identify discipline strategies/alternative parent behavior options for handling the situation.

Self-Help Worksheet for Managing Parental Anger

1. What happened/the situation.

2. What I thought to myself that did *not* help me handle the situation.

3. How I felt.

4. What my behavior looked like.

5. What I can think to myself to help me handle the situation better.

6. How I can feel.

7. What my behavior can look like.

8. Discipline strategies/alternative parent behavior options for handling the situation.

Self-Help Worksheet for Managing Parental Anger

1. What happened/the situation.

2. What I thought to myself that did *not* help me handle the situation.

3. How I felt.

4. What my behavior looked like.

5. What I can think to myself to help me handle the situation better.

6. How I can feel.

7. What my behavior can look like.

8. Discipline strategies/alternative parent behavior options for handling the situation.

Self-Help Worksheet for Managing Parental Anger: Newborn Example

1. **What happened/the situation.**
   I tried to calm the baby down and he's still crying. I put him in the playpen and he's still wailing.

2. **What I thought to myself that did not help me handle the situation.**
   I hate it when he does this. He's doing it on purpose. Why can't I calm him? I can't stand this.

3. **How I felt.**
   Angry
   Depressed

4. **What my behavior looked like.**
   Impatient
   Short and abrupt
   Yelling

5. **What I can think to myself to help me handle the situation better.**
   Babies are fussy and uncooperative. PERIOD. I'm not always going to be able to comfort him. It's not realistic.

6. **How I can feel.**
   Tolerant but somewhat frustrated

7. **What my behavior can look like.**
   Matter-of-fact
   Reassuring and supportive but firm

8. **Discipline strategies/alternative parent behavior options for handling the situation.**
   I can check for signs of illness or discomfort which I may be able to deal with. I can put the baby in his bed or playpen and let him fall asleep or at least calm down before I pick him up again.

Self-Help Worksheet for Managing Parental Anger: Infant Example

1. **What happened/the situation.**
   *My baby puts cereal in her hair every time
   I feed her.*

2. **What I thought to myself that did not
   help me handle the situation.**
   *I said stop it! Look at the mess! I teach you
   and why can't you learn? I can't stand this.
   This is serious.*

3. **How I felt.**
   *Angry
   Depressed*

4. **What my behavior looked like.**
   *Short and gruff, making mealtime unpleasant
   for my baby and me.*

5. **What I can think to myself to help me
   handle the situation better.**
   *She's just exploring her food and then touching her
   head. She's made messes before and I've stood it,
   even though I don't like it. It's not a disaster.*

6. **How I can feel.**
   *Frustrated and perhaps a little amused
   Tolerant*

7. **What my behavior can look like.**
   *Low keyed and matter-of-fact
   but firm where needed*

8. **Discipline strategies/alternative parent
   behavior options for handling the situation.**
   *When she starts putting food in her hair I can say "No,"
   and remove her from her chair for a moment. I can give her
   a spoon or toy to hold and mess up with food. I can give
   her a finger food to hold while I spoon feed. I can put a
   shower cap on her until the meal is over.*

Self-Help Worksheet for Managing Parental Anger: Toddler Example

1. **What happened/the situation.**
   My child put his hairbrush in the toilet and flushed it. The bathroom flooded!

2. **What I thought to myself that did not help me handle the situation.**
   I can't believe it. He knows better. I can't stand it when you do these things. It'll cost a lot to fix it.

3. **How I felt.**
   Angry!
   Intolerant of frustration

4. **What my behavior looked like.**
   I spanked.
   I screamed.
   I yelled.

5. **What I can think to myself to help me handle the situation better.**
   What a mess — some days are like this. Maybe I can fix it. I better do some training on what to put in the toilet.

6. **How I can feel.**
   Annoyed

7. **What my behavior can look like.**
   Firm, but not out of control

8. **Discipline strategies/alternative parent behavior options for handling the situation.**
   I can say "NO" and remove the child to a safe place for quiet time and discipline while I clean up. I can secure the bathroom doors when he's playing around. I can show him only what he can flush.

Self-Help Worksheet for Managing Parental Anger: Toddler Example

1. **What happened/the situation.**
   Every time I try to change his diaper, he squirms and makes the task next to impossible.

2. **What I thought to myself that did *not* help me handle the situation.**
   Don't you know you need changing? I hate this, cooperate! Why can't you hold still? Change your own diaper!

3. **How I felt.**
   Angry
   Intolerant of frustration

4. **What my behavior looked like.**
   Short, gruff, yelling
   Rough with him

5. **What I can think to myself to help me handle the situation better.**
   It certainly makes changing more tricky, but it can be done. We'll get through this — we have many times before.

6. **How I can feel.**
   Tolerant but somewhat frustrated and annoyed

7. **What my behavior can look like.**
   Firm but matter-of-fact

8. **Discipline strategies/alternative parent behavior options for handling the situation.**
   I can give him something to hold while I change him. I can put him next to a mirror to talk to himself. I can put him on the floor so he won't roll off the changing table. I can change him and then reward him in some way so he comes to learn it's fun time.

Self-Help Worksheet for Managing Parental Anger: Childhood Example

1. **What happened/the situation.**
   When my child accompanies me to the grocery store, he demands candy to eat now.

2. **What I thought to myself that did *not* help me handle the situation.**
   Doesn't he know I'm in a hurry? He shouldn't always demand things. I can't stand it when he's like this.

3. **How I felt.**
   Angry
   Intolerant of frustration

4. **What my behavior looked like.**
   Yelling
   Curt and critical

5. **What I can think to myself to help me handle the situation better.**
   Kids are normally self-centered and want things. Just because he asked, doesn't mean I have to give. He has done this before. I can deal with it even though I don't like it.

6. **How I can feel.**
   Annoyed but tolerant
   Mildly frustrated

7. **What my behavior can look like.**
   Educative, firm, assertive, patient

8. **Discipline strategies/alternative parent behavior options for handling the situation.**
   I can structure th situation before we go and tell the child we are only shopping for groceries for meals. I can say firmly, "I understand your feelings of disappointment but this time we will be unable to buy candy as I told you before we left." I can teach them patience by saying, "First, we will get groceries then we will get your treat if you don't keep asking for it."

Self-Help Worksheet for Managing Parental Anger: Middle Childhood Example

1. **What happened/the situation.**
   My son didn't clean his room as I asked.

2. **What I thought to myself that did *not* help me handle the situation.**
   How dare he ignore me and leave without doing it. Who does he think he is? I can't stand this. What a pig! Wait until I catch up with him!

3. **How I felt.**
   Angry!
   Intolerant of frustration

4. **What my behavior looked like.**
   Screamed and yelled and berated him

5. **What I can think to myself to help me handle the situation better.**
   Kids don't always accept responsibility. They frequently take the easy way out. My standards of orderliness aren't shared by all. I'll get the rule across another way. I won't die from the mess.

6. **How I can feel.**
   Matter-of-fact with no anger, but concerned
   Possibly annoyed

7. **What my behavior can look like.**
   Firm and to-the-point

8. **Discipline strategies/alternative parent behavior options for handling the situation.**
   I can restate the rule and emphasize his responsibility. I can tell him it's to be done first before he can have other privileges. I can tell him I appreciate it when he keeps up his end of responsibilities. I can close his door so I won't look at it until he gets it done.

Self-Help Worksheet for Managing Parental Anger: Middle Childhood Example

1. **What happened/the situation.**
   My daughter traded a neighbor child Aunt Martha's heirloom locket for a scatch 'n sniff sticker.

2. **What I thought to myself that did *not* help me handle the situation.**
   How could you! How dare you trade something that doesn't belong to you. I can't stand it when you do these things.

3. **How I felt.**
   Angry
   Intolerant of frustration

4. **What my behavior looked like.**
   Yelled and screamed
   Berated her

5. **What I can think to myself to help me handle the situation better.**
   Part of growing up is making mistakes; there will be lots of them. Children don't always understand the material or sentimental worth of things.

6. **How I can feel.**
   Annoyed

7. **What my behavior can look like.**
   Firm, educative, patient

8. **Discipline strategies/alternative parent behavior options for handling the situation.**
   I can involve the child in correcting the mistake. I can teach the concepts of similar value, material value and sentimental value. I can provide a consequence of adding something bad like an extra chore or taking away something good like a privilege to show disapproval. I can point out what other trades she could have made which would have been more reasonable.

Self-Help Worksheet for Managing Parental Anger: Teenage Example

1. **What happened/the situation.**
   My child continually says he has no homework and at the parent-teacher meeting I was told my child will always have some homework.

2. **What I thought to myself that did not help me handle the situation.**
   How dare he lie to me! He must think I'm stupid and he can get away with this. He should know this is hurting him and is irresponsible. What must the teacher think of me?

3. **How I felt.**
   Angry
   Worried
   Frustrated
   Embarrassed

4. **What my behavior looked like.**
   Argumentative
   Confrontive
   Cutting down the child as a person
   Overly punitive

5. **What I can think to myself to help me handle the situation better.**
   Sometimes kids take the easy way out and are not truthful about their homework. Not all kids at this age are self-motivated and disciplined. Many kids at this age don't see past today. Not doing his homework does not make me a bad parent.

6. **How I can feel.**
   Concerned

7. **What my behavior can look like.**
   Educative, firm but patient, encouraging

8. **Discipline strategies/alternative parent behavior options for handling the situation.**
   I can set up with my child a regular study time whether or not he has homework. I can request a weekly progress report from school until he is consistently on track. I can request a teacher conference with my child to make him aware that his choices are affecting his grades. I can work out a reward/contract with my child to encourage him to complete his work and turn it in. I can provide a punishment of limited duration so that it makes a point of disapproval and provides a consequence that does not leave the teen feeling hopelessly limited and rebellious.

Self-Help Worksheet for Managing Parental Anger: Teenage Example

1. **What happened/the situation.**
   I let my son use the family car and he came home without the gas cap.

2. **What I thought to myself that did not help me handle the situation.**
   What a screw-up! Can't you take care of anything! I can't stand it when I give you a privilege and you abuse it!

3. **How I felt.**
   Angry
   Intolerant of frustration

4. **What my behavior looked like.**
   Yelled and screamed
   Grounded him for 6 months

5. **What I can think to myself to help me handle the situation better.**
   Anyone can lose a gas cap. Just because he screwed up doesn't make him a screw-up. This won't be the first or last time he makes a mistake. I want to get the responsibility issue across, not my anger.

6. **How I can feel.**
   Annoyed

7. **What my behavior can look like.**
   Firm
   Matter-of-fact

8. **Discipline strategies/alternative parent behavior options for handling the situation.**
   I can help him recreate his activities to help him figure out where he may have left it and then help him track it down and get it. If it's lost, I can have him price a new one and purchase it with his money.

Self-Help Worksheet for Managing Parental Anger: Teenage Example

1. **What happened/the situation.**
   My daughter went out and promised to be home on time. She came home 1 hour late.

2. **What I thought to myself that did *not* help me handle the situation.**
   How dare she defy me. I won't stand for this. She should always be home on time. What if something happened to her? What if she was in an accident?

3. **How I felt.**
   Angry
   Worried

4. **What my behavior looked like.**
   Yelled and screamed
   Grounded her for a long period of time

5. **What I can think to myself to help me handle the situation better.**
   Sometimes lateness is unavoidable; I want her to know how to handle it. It's unacceptable to be late. She made a judgment error, but she's not a bad person. I don't want this to become a pattern.

6. **How I can feel.**
   Annoyed and concerned

7. **What my behavior can look like.**
   Firm

8. **Discipline strategies/alternative parent behavior options for handling the situation.**
   I can let her know this is not acceptable and won't be condoned by restricting the privilege for a time. If it was unavoidable, I want her to know how to handle it so I won't worry myself.

Chapter 4

Anger: Helping Myself, My Spouse, And My Children Manage Anger Better

Helping My Spouse Replace Non-Helpful Thoughts With Helpful Ones.

It is desirable for me to help my spouse replace non-helpful thoughts with helpful ones.

Because one of the key aspects of these techniques is learning to become aware of and modifying your own thoughts, you can begin managing your own anger by yourself. Seeing the progress in your parenting behavior — the undesirable disappearing — can act like a reward and further motivation to self-improvement.

If you are part of a two-parent family, you can work on improved parenting together. Provide encouragement to your spouse when you see him or her handling a situation well (though perhaps not perfectly). Sometimes it's helpful to work out a signal system for "anger approaching" between the two of you (STOP—THINK—ACT could be the cue phrase). Occasionally, review together your individual warning signals. Examples might include early aware-

31

ness of physiological changes such as butterflies in your stomach, tightness in your chest or around your head, increased heart rate, or facial flushing. Early awareness of behavioral changes might include teeth gnashing, fist clinching, fist pounding, increases in voice volume, finger pointing, or the use of "trigger" words or phrases such as profanities.

Sometimes — after the situation has passed **and** your spouse is no longer angry — you might say aloud, gently but firmly, whatever hurtful self-statement you think your spouse was using. Often, after the anger has passed, your spouse will be better able to recognize how the non-helpful self-statements were related to the upset.

Modeling Helpful Thoughts For My Children.

It is desirable in selected situations for me to model helpful thoughts aloud for my children to hear so that they may learn to be more helpful to themselves.

Much of a child's learning occurs through imitation; children often copy behavior that they have observed. If you say aloud, in certain situations, helpful statements to your children, your children may learn to use those statements to help themselves in similar situations.

For example, let's say you have begun to stop rating your worth and are, instead, rating your performance in a situation. You might say something like this: "The fact that I made a mistake does not mean that I am a mistake as a person. When I do something inappropriate, my behavior was inappropriate — I am not a bad person. Everyone makes mistakes. I can stand making mistakes."

Many parents would like to be able to teach such lessons to their children. The lessons can be learned by copying. When you see your children using helpful self-statements or handling situations better, reinforce the process by noting and commending their coping behavior.

Becoming More Skillful By Practicing.

I will become more skillful at overcoming my anger if I practice every day.

Managing parental anger is a responsibility. It is one you assume not only for the sake of your children, but for your own sake. If you are willing to accept the responsibility for your own upset, you will be better able to control your upsets and to parent effectively.

People are creatures of learned habits. Habits, though often stubborn, can be changed. If you can replace the time spent making yourself angry, or being non-educative with your children, or stewing over bad feelings about parenting, with time spent learning how to manage parental anger, you will — at the very least — spend your valuable time more wisely.

Every time you behave more skillfully as a parent is a victory. With practice, you can add more victories to the lives of your children and to your own life.

Chapter 5

Discipline: Being More Effective
At Managing Behavior

Discipline Without Anger

When I discipline without anger, I can enjoy parenting more and I can be more effective in teaching my children what is appropriate and inappropriate behavior.

1. I will be better able to review my options for handling the misbehavior.
2. My children will not be as likely to withdraw from me because of my angry outbursts.
3. My children will be able to look at their misbehavior and take responsibility for it if they are provided a negative consequence.

Helpful Guidelines For Good Discipline

Most parents think that discipline and punishment are the same thing. On a day-to-day basis, many parents try to discipline by punishing.

The dictionary, however, defines discipline as "training to produce a specific pattern of behavior." If we want to teach our children **what not to do**, it seems appropriate to train them **what to do**.

Punishment (following an inappropriate action with a negative consequence) will cause the misbehavior to decrease — the child has learned what not to do.

Reinforcement (following an appropriate action with a positive consequence) tells children what to do. If reinforcement works for a particular child, the consequence will cause the behavior to increase — the child has learned what to do.

If children are trained with punishment, they are taught what things not to do. Through a trial and error or a gradual elimination process, they may figure out what their parents want them to do. It seems a shame to leave a child's learning to chance.

The following guidelines are suggested for more effective discipline:

1. Be SPECIFIC about the behavior you punish or encourage. Identify the act instead of calling it "your behavior" or "**that** was" or "**it** is…" Specify behaviors this way: "Taking the book without asking first is unacceptable." "I like the way you asked for the book before taking it." "Biting your sister is unacceptable." "I like the way you are taking turns."

2. Be IMMEDIATE when providing a negative or positive consequence for behavior. Providing a consequence right after the incident is much more effective than bringing up the issue five minutes or five hours later. Accomplishing this means keeping on top of your children's behavior and giving them frequent feedback.

3. Consequences only work as punishers if they decrease the probability of future occurrence of the inappropriate behavior; they only work as reinforcers if they increase the probability of future occurrence of appropriate behavior. What you think is a positive or negative consequence may not work quite that way for your children.

When your consequence does not work — time after time — you may decide your child is simply unmanageable, but this is not necessarily so. The problem may be that you have not yet found the consequence that works with your child, or maybe your technique in using the consequence is faulty. A list of suggested readings in child management and parenting at the end of this book may give you some specific ideas about techniques in applying consequence.

4. Direct the consequence at the behavior, **not** at the child or the

child's worth. You are trying to encourage or discourage **behavior**. This is important to remember.

You may be asking yourself what could possibly be wrong with saying to my child, "I am pleased with you for what you did and you are a good child." There are a couple of problems with this statement. One of the problems with this message is that it tells the child that personal worth is directly related to doing those things that you, the parent, have deemed appropriate. What you want to teach your child is that they have worth as human beings, their actions may be evaluated by others, and the evaluation of their actions and their human worth are two separate and distinct things, and are not to be confused.

Assigning worth to a child based on how they perform or act can be questioned as setting the child up to believe that if he or she behaves correctly then he or she can be rated as being more worthwhile. There is no real method for proving human worth or value and there are disadvantages such as self-downing to connecting worth with performance. With kids it is preferable to connect behavior as leading to greater happiness or unhappiness for the child without putting the child's worth on the line. Thus, if a child does well in school, that makes the parents happy and the child may be pleased regarding his or her performance. However, it is also not a commentary on the child's worth if he or she does poorly in school but rather an indication that the child's school **performance** is lacking.

If you do not separate the issues of worth and actions for your children, you are open to another big problem; if your children believe they are good and you love them and are proud of them because of their good deeds, then they may well see themselves as bad, worthless and unloved when they misbehave. This is a tragically disproportionate seed to plant in children's minds. How much healthier it is for a child to make a mistake, meet the consequences, and learn from both. How much better that than feeling rejected and less worthy for having made a mistake.

5. Whenever possible, use a predetermined rule when disciplining. If you see your child following such a rule, you may say something like, "I like the way you are putting your toys away before taking out another one." If the child is doing something inappropriate, you might say something like, "The rule is you put away your toy before you take another."

You are suggesting to the child that life has rules and you are

37

organized enough to know what they are. The likelihood of consistently enforcing a rule is greater, too, if you have that rule firm in your own mind. And, reminding the child of a rule instead of saying, "I said" or "Mommy said" removes you from the kind of stand-off that can easily develop into a power struggle.

6. Frequently use the term "First...then" in allowing your child to do something. This technique allows the parent to stay in control. It also reduces the "demandingness" children can get into. If Bill says, "Give me a drink, please," you say, "Thank you for saying 'please' so nicely, Billy — **first** you get me a paper cup, **then** I will pour your drink."

7. Model good behavior patterns, allow your child to imitate them, and praise his or her good behavior.

Chapter 6

Conclusion

As you use the suggested guidelines for discipline you will find they are more effective when used without anger. Your children will be more able to be positively encouraged or negatively discouraged without the interference of reacting to **your** anger.

Throughout this book it has been suggested that anger isn't useful in dealing with children; they can be dealt with more effectively without anger. Yet you will still get angry at times even if you try to use the ideas in this book. The reason you will get angry is that like all human beings you are fallible. Fallible means imperfect and mistake-prone. All of us make errors, mistakes in judgment, and lack perfect control of our emotions. While it is important to work very hard on reducing your anger, it is likely you will still express it occasionally. Hopefully your anger will, with hard work, occur less frequently, be less intense, and not last as long.

It is important to accept your fallibility so when you don't do well with your anger you do not become self-downing and angry with yourself. Kicking yourself around in the dust will not improve your performance as a parent the next time around. If you perform poorly and get angry, accept the responsibility for your anger while accepting your fallibility as a person. Try to learn what you could have done differently by reviewing a self-help worksheet. Once you've completed the self-help worksheet and thought about how you could improve your performance in a similar future situation and you've done everything you can do to improve, it's time to forget your upset and move on.

Most adults find that the change from a parent who gets angry quickly to a parent who controls their anger is gradual, not immediate. Whenever you notice that you are getting angry, use one of the techniques from this book. Over a period of time you will notice your anger sooner and sooner in the progression, allowing you to avoid a good deal of anger altogether.

Finally, you would do best to keep in mind that the suggested ideas in this book will work best if you work very hard in the ways suggested to use them. Without much effort on your part your hurtful thoughts that lead to anger will dominate. As you work at using the suggested ideas, don't forget to encourage your efforts by giving yourself praise for even the smallest changes.

Suggested Readings

The following books may be helpful in giving you additional help in the topical areas listed. These readings will give you more ideas for applications in your life and with your children. Further they will encourage ideas covered in this book. The suggested readings are listed topically to give you a more specific idea of which book will be most helpful to your needs.

COPING SKILLS

Burns, D.D. (1981). **Feeling Good: The New Mood Therapy.** New York: William Morrow & Co.

*Ellis, A., & Harper, R.A. (1961). **A New Guide to Rational Living.** Englewood Cliffs, NJ: Prentice-Hall.

*Ellis, A. (1988). **How to Stubbornly Refuse to be Ashamed of Anything.** Secaucus, NJ: Lyle Stuart.

*Ellis, A. (1977). **Conquering Low Frustration Tolerance** (cassette recording). New York: Institute for Rational Living.

*Ellis, A. (1977). **How to Live-With-and-Without-Anger.** New York: Reader's Digest Press.

*Ellis, A. & Becker, I. (1982). **A Guide to Personal Happiness.** Hollywood, CA: Wilshire Book Co.

RATIONAL EMOTIVE THERAPY — COGNITIVE THERAPY

Beck, A.T. (1976). **Cognitive Therapy and the Emotional Disorders.** New York: International Universities Press.

*Ellis, A. (1962). **Reason and Emotion in Psychotherapy.** New York: Lyle Stuart.

*Ellis, A., & Grieger, R. (1977). **A Handbook of Rational-Emotive Therapy.** New York: Springer.

*Ellis, A. (1979). A Rational-Emotive Approach to Family Therapy: Part 2. **Rational Living** 14 (1), 23-27.

Mahoney, M.J. (1974). **Cognitive-Behavior Modification.** Cambridge, MA: Ballinger.

Meichenbaum, D.H. (1974). **Cognitive-Behavior Modification.** Morristown, NJ: General Learning Press.

*Walen, S., DiGiuseppe, R., & Wessler, R. (1980). **A Practitioner's Guide to Rational Emotive Therapy.** New York: Oxford University Press.

*Wessler, R.A., & Wessler, R.S. (1980). **The Principles and Practice of Rational-Emotive Therapy.** San Francisco, CA: Jossey-Bass.

GENERAL PARENTING — DISCIPLINE

Barrish, H.H., & Barrish, I.J. (1989). **Surviving and Enjoying Your Adolescent.** Kansas City, MO: Westport Publishers.

Becker, W.C. (1972). **Parents are Teachers.** Champaign, IL: Research Press.

Christophersen, E.R. (1988). **Little People: Guidelines for Commonsense Child Rearing** (3rd ed.). Kansas City, MO: Westport Publishers.

Hauck, P. (1975). **The Rational Management of Children.** New York: Libra.

Patterson, G.R. (1972). **Living with Children.** Champaign, IL: Research Press.

Patterson, G.R. (1974). **Families.** Champaign, IL: Research Press.

Silberman, M.L., & Wheelan, A. (1980). **How to Discipline Without Feeling Guilty.** Champaign, IL: Research Press.

Wycoff, J., & Unell, B.C. (1984). **Discipline Without Shouting or Spanking.** New York: Simon & Schuster.

RATIONAL EMOTIVE THERAPY IN EDUCATION

*Knaus, W.J. (1974). **Rational-Emotive Education: A Manual for Elementary School Teachers.** New York: Institute for Rational Living.

*These books or tapes can be ordered from the Institute for Rational-Emotive Therapy, 45 East 65th St., New York, NY 10021.

About the Authors

Harriet H. Barrish, Ph.D. is a licensed psychologist in private practice in Leawood, Kansas.

Dr. Barrish works extensively with parents, families and women in both educational and clinical settings. She is an Associate Fellow of the Institute for Rational-Emotive Therapy in New York and a member of the National Register of Health Service Providers in Psychology.

She is also a past president of the Kansas Psychological Association.

———————————————

I.J. Barrish, Ph.D. is a Behavioral and Developmental Child Psychologist who is in private practice in Leawood, Kansas.

Dr. Barrish works extensively with children, adolescents, adults and families in both educational and clinical settings.

Dr. Barrish is also an Associate Fellow and Supervisor of the Institute for Rational-Emotive Therapy in New York.

ORDER DIRECT: 1-800-347-BOOK

❑ YES, I want _____ copies of
Managing and Understanding Parental Anger
for $6.95 each plus $2 shipping.

❑ YES, I want _____ copies of
Surviving and Enjoying Your Adolescent
for $7.95 each plus $2 shipping.

❑ Check enclosed for $_____ payable to:
Westport Publishers • 4050 Pennsylvania Ave.
Suite 310 • Kansas City, MO 64111

❑ Charge my credit card: ☐ Visa ☐ MasterCard
Acct. #_____ Exp. Date _____
Signature_____

SHIP TO: _____
_____
_____

ORDER DIRECT: 1-800-347-BOOK

❑ YES, I want _____ copies of
Managing and Understanding Parental Anger
for $6.95 each plus $2 shipping.

❑ YES, I want _____ copies of
Surviving and Enjoying Your Adolescent
for $7.95 each plus $2 shipping.

❑ Check enclosed for $_____ payable to:
Westport Publishers • 4050 Pennsylvania Ave.
Suite 310 • Kansas City, MO 64111

❑ Charge my credit card: ☐ Visa ☐ MasterCard
Acct. #_____ Exp. Date _____
Signature_____

SHIP TO: _____
_____
_____

Westport Publishers
4050 Pennsylvania Ave.
Suite 310
Kansas City, MO 64111

Westport Publishers
4050 Pennsylvania Ave.
Suite 310
Kansas City, MO 64111